Word Problems Booster

Word Problems Booster provides focused practice to help reinforce and develop their ability to solve word problems. Problems are grade-level appropriate with clear examples. In accordance with national standards, exercises for grade four focus on math skills such as addition, subtraction, multiplication, division, estimation, geometry, graphing, money values, fractions, measurement, and decimals.

Word Problems Booster is fact filled and fast paced to keep learning interesting, fun, and exciting while students improve their ability to do math.

For information, write: Skill Mill • PO Box 571470 • Salt Lake City, Utah 84157-1470.

Please visit our website at
www.skillmill.com
for supplements, additions, and corrections to this book.

First Edition 2003

ISBN: 1-932210-41-5

PRINTED IN THE UNITED STATES OF AMERICA
10 9 8 7 6 5 4 3 2 1

Table of Contents

A Bug's Life

Solve each problem.

1. Anita saw 25 grasshoppers and 16 beetles in the field. How many grasshoppers and beetles did Anita see altogether?

$$\begin{array}{r} {\overset{1}{2}5} \\ + 16 \\ \hline 41 \end{array}\text{ bugs}$$

2. Charley counted 19 more black ants than red ants. Charley counted 34 red ants. How many black ants did Charley count?

3. There were 28 more caterpillars in the flower garden than in the vegetable garden. If there were 31 caterpillars in the vegetable garden, how many caterpillars were there in the flower garden?

4. Eric counted 13 black spiders and 48 brown spiders. How many spiders did Eric count altogether?

Bugs are so cool!

5. Jill saw 29 ladybugs in the orchard and 14 ladybugs near the patio. How many ladybugs did Jill see in all?

Solve each problem.

1. Jackson fed the penguins 342 pounds of food in March. In May, Jackson fed the penguins 489 pounds of food. How many pounds of food did Jackson feed the penguins total?

    $$\begin{array}{r} \overset{1\,1}{342} \\ +\ 489 \\ \hline 831 \end{array}$$ **pounds of food**

2. Laura counted 14 green lizards, 35 snakes, and 48 chameleons. How many reptiles did she see in all?

3. On Monday, 2,492 people visited the zoo. On Saturday, 4,399 people visited the zoo. How many people visited the zoo on Monday and Saturday altogether?

4. Alex took 34 pictures of bears, 29 pictures of cats, and 48 pictures of reptiles. How many pictures did Alex take altogether?

5. Keshia talks to the zookeeper about what the zoo's birds are fed. The birds ate 3,295 ounces of birdseed in the spring and 2,945 ounces of birdseed in the summer. How many ounces of birdseed did the birds eat in the spring and summer combined?

www.skillmill.com

1-932210-41-5

Solve each problem.

1. Adam saw 15 bees in the flowers. Later, Adam saw 22 bees in the flowers. How many bees did Adam see altogether?

2. Marcy saw 21 more butterflies than Jim saw. Jim saw 19 butterflies. How many butterflies did Marcy see?

3. Andy cleaned 45 cages on Monday, 36 cages on Tuesday and 69 cages on Wednesday. How many cages did Andy clean altogether?

4. Lisa walked 72 feet to see the leopards, 129 feet to see the alligators, and 218 feet to see the monkeys. How many feet did Lisa walk in all?

5. The zoo has 148 reptiles, 28 mammals, and 69 birds. How many animals does the zoo have altogether?

Did you know?

In the U.S., 14 reptiles are on the endangered species list. The American crocodile, found in Florida, is among them.

How Tall?

Solve each problem.

1. The tallest giant sequoia tree is 275 feet. The tallest coastal red-wood tree is 321 feet. How much taller is the coastal redwood tree than the giant sequoia tree?

$$\begin{array}{r} 2\overset{1}{}11 \\ \cancel{321} \\ -\ 275 \\ \hline 46 \end{array}$$ **feet taller**

2. The Sears Tower in Chicago is 1,450 feet tall. The John Hancock Center in Chicago is 1,127 feet tall. How much taller is the Sears Tower than the John Hancock Center?

3. The tallest sugar pine tree is 232 feet. The tallest western red cedar tree is 159 feet. How much taller is the sugar pine than the western red cedar?

4. The Empire State Building is 1,250 feet tall. The Chrysler Building is 1,046 feet tall. How much taller is the Empire State Building than the Chrysler Building?

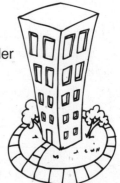

Did you know?

The oldest living tree is in California. It is a bristlecone pine tree named Methuselah and is estimated to be 4,700 years old.

www.skillmill.com   1-932210-41-5

Solve each problem.

1. The highest temperature in Duluth, Minnesota, was 97° F. The highest temperature in Barrow, Alaska, was 79° F. How much warmer was Duluth than Barrow?

$$\begin{array}{r} \overset{8\,1}{\cancel{9}\cancel{7}}° \\ -\ 79° \\ \hline 18°\ \textbf{warmer} \end{array}$$

2. Seattle, Washington, received 37 inches of rain in a year. Jackson, Mississippi, had 55 inches of rain. How much more rain did Jackson get than Seattle?

3. The maximum normal temperature in January for Houston, Texas, is 61° F. Rapid City, South Dakota, has a maximum normal temperature of 34° F in January. How much colder is Rapid City than Houston?

4. The weather station in Baltimore, Maryland, reported its fastest wind at 41 miles per hour. Fairbanks, Alaska, reported its fastest wind at 26 miles per hour. How much faster was the wind that was reported in Baltimore?

Did you know?

The hottest temperature recorded in the U.S. was 134° F. It was recorded in Death Valley, CA, on July 10, 1913. The coldest temperature recorded in the U.S. was -80° F. It was recorded a Prospect Creek, AK, on January 23, 1971.

7

Solve each problem.

1. Alexis sold 1,223 cups of Fizzy Cola. Sam sold 873 cups. How many cups of Fizzy Cola did Alexis and Sam sell altogether?

$$^{1}1,223$$
$$+ \ \ 873$$
$$2,096 \textbf{ cups}$$

2. In January, the theater sold 5,685 movie tickets. The theater sold 183 more movie tickets in March than in January. How many tickets were sold in March?

3. Bill sold 127 boxes of Starblast candy and 839 packages of licorice. How many more packages of licorice than Starblast candy did Bill sell?

4. During the opening week of *Space Survivors*, the theater sold 1,386 tickets. The theater sold 884 tickets during the opening week of *Creatures from Orb*. How many more tickets were sold in the opening week of *Space Survivors*?

5. The ShowTime Theater has 1,253 seats. The Cinemania Theater has 784 seats. How many more seats does the ShowTime Theater have than the Cinemania Theater?

www.skillmill.com   1-932210-41-5

Under the Sea

Solve each problem.

1. Divers saw 432 tropical fish on their first dive, 289 tropical fish on their second dive, and 637 tropical fish on their third dive. How many tropical fish did they see altogether?

1 1
432
289
+ 637
1,358 tropical fish

2. The Pacific Ocean has an average depth of 12,925 feet. The Gulf of Mexico has an average depth of 5,297 feet. What is the difference in average depth between the Gulf of Mexico and the Pacific Ocean?

3. Misha collected 1,946 seashells. Abe collected 3,479 seashells. How many seashells did Misha and Abe collect in all?

4. A blue whale traveled 1,349 feet the first time it was sighted. The second time it was sighted, the blue whale had traveled another 977 feet. How far did the blue whale travel altogether?

5. A scientist observed 423 sea urchins on his first trip. On his second trip, the scientist observed 296 sea urchins. How many more sea urchins did the scientist observe on his first trip than on his second trip?

I see the fish under the sea!

1-932210-41-5

Word Problems—Grade 4

Solve each problem.

1. Both the Mauna Loa and Kilauea volcanoes are in Hawaii. The Mauna Loa volcano is 13,680 feet tall. The Kilauea volcano is 4,190 feet tall. How much taller is the Mauna Loa volcano than the Kilauea volcano?

2. Mt. Everest, the world's tallest mountain, is 29,035 feet tall. Mt. McKinley is 20,320 feet tall. How much taller is Mt. Everest than Mt. McKinley?

3. The California laurel tree is 108 feet tall. The sitka spruce tree is 191 feet tall. How much taller is the sitka spruce than the California laurel?

4. Jason saw 42 octopi, 142 crabs, and 339 fish. How many sea creatures did he see altogether?

5. Leslie saw 1,228 fewer fish than Taylor. Taylor saw 3,212 fish. How many fish did Leslie see?

6. The dolphin swims 1,268 feet. The shark swims 3,145 feet. How much farther does the shark swim than the dolphin?

Time for Tunes

Lisa's class took a poll at their school. They asked students what type of music they liked best. Use the results below to answer the questions that follow.

1. How many total students like pop music or country music?

$$\begin{array}{r} {\scriptstyle 1\ 1\ 1} \\ 3{,}493 \\ +\ 1{,}998 \\ \hline 5{,}491 \text{ students} \end{array}$$

Rosewood School's Favorite Music Poll	
Rock	4,755 students
Pop	3,493 students
Country	1,998 students
Rap	1,043 students
Jazz	845 students
Oldies	391 students
Classical	173 students

2. How many more students like rap music than jazz music?

3. How many total students like oldies music or classical music?

4. More students like rock music than pop music. How many more students like rock music?

5. How many students like jazz music or oldies music altogether?

6. How many more students like pop music than country music?

1-932210-41-5
Word Problems—Grade 4

Gathering Groceries

Use the price list below to answer each question.

1. Eric's mom wants him to buy 1 gallon of milk and 3 boxes of cereal. How much money does he need?

$$\begin{array}{r} {\scriptstyle 1\ 1} \\ \$2.89 \\ +\ \underline{\$10.79} \\ \$13.68 \end{array}$$

Grocery List

1 bag of carrots	$1.79
1 package of grapes	$2.47
2 pounds of chicken	$6.62
1 gallon of milk	$2.89
3 loaves of bread	$3.58
8 cups of yogurt	$4.27
1 package of cheese	$5.59
3 boxes of cereal	$10.79
1 package of gum	$.76

2. Kendra buys 1 package of cheese. She pays for the cheese with a ten-dollar bill. How much change will Kendra get back?

3. Daniel buys 8 cups of yogurt and 3 loaves of bread. How much does Daniel spend altogether?

4. Kim has $15.25. She buys 2 pounds of chicken. How much does she have left?

5. Marc buys 1 package of grapes and 3 loaves of bread. His little sister wants a package of gum. Marc only has $7.00 in his wallet. Does he have enough money to buy the gum?

www.skillmill.com   1-932210-41-5

Collecting Collectibles

Solve each problem.

1. Hank collects stamps. He buys a rare stamp for $71.93 and a package of stamps for $14.37. How much does Hank spend on stamps?

    $$\begin{array}{r} {}^{1\ 1}\\ \$71.93 \\ + \ \$14.37 \\ \hline \$86.30 \end{array}$$

2. At the toy store, Jill spends $95.38 for a doll. Carrie spends $42.69 less than Jill for a doll. How much does Carrie spend?

3. Hector buys a model car for $24.98. Then he spends $18.39 on supplies to build the model car. How much does Hector spend altogether?

4. Mike collects baseball cards. He spends $58.27 on a rookie card. Then he spends $74.93 on his favorite pitcher's card. How much does Mike spend on baseball cards in all?

5. Jack collects aluminum cans for recycling. He earns $23.79 in March and $39.08 in April. How much more money did Jack earn in April than in March?

Did you know?

If you had 10 billion $1 bills and spent one every second of every day, it would take 317 years for you to go broke.

Solve each problem using the information in the table.

FOOD ITEMS	CALORIES
applesauce 194	
celery 9	
chicken noodle soup 75	
chocolate chip cookies 226	
hamburger 369	
milk 95	
orange 65	
peanut butter sandwich 334	
pizza (1 slice) 378	

1. James eats an orange, a peanut butter sandwich, and a glass of milk for lunch. How many calories does James eat?

$$\begin{array}{r} \overset{1}{65} \\ \overset{1}{334} \\ + \ 95 \\ \hline \textbf{494} \end{array}$$ **calories**

2. How many more calories does one slice of pizza have than a peanut butter sandwich?

3. If Lisa eats a hamburger and one serving of celery for lunch, how many calories does she eat?

4. After school, Amber has chocolate chip cookies and a glass of milk for a snack. How many calories does she eat?

Tuna on rye—my favorite!

5. For lunch, Daniel orders a bowl of chicken noodle soup, applesauce and chocolate chip cookies. How many calories are in his lunch?

6. What food item in the table has the most calories?

www.skillmill.com

1-932210-41-5

Solve each problem.

1. John buys a painting for his collection. He spends $83.67. He gives the clerk $100.00. How much money does he get back?

2. Anne and Jim collect watches. Anne buys a watch for $58.48. Jim pays $39.37 more for his watch. How much does Jim pay?

3. Maria collects stickers. She spends $2.93 at the first store. She spends $12.43 at the second store. How much does Maria spend altogether?

4. In July, Los Angeles, California's, highest temperature was 84° F. Its lowest temperature during the same month was 65° F. What was the difference between its highest and lowest temperature?

5. The ShowTime Theater has 962 tickets available for Monday night. They sell 543 tickets. How many tickets do they have left?

Did you know?

According to the official census, the U.S. population in 2000 was 281,421,906. California is the state with the largest population.

1-932210-41-5
Word Problems—Grade 4

People Populations

Round each number to the nearest ten, hundred, or thousand.

Remember... When you round numbers, look at the number that follows the number you are rounding. For example, when rounding to the nearest ten, if the number you are rounding is followed by 5 or more, you round the number up. If the number you are rounding is followed by 4 or less, you round the number down.

1. In Ashley's school there are 42 students who have computers.

   42 rounded to the nearest 10 = **40**

2. The chess club has 39 members.

3. In Jay's class, 24 students like to go bowling.

Round each number to the nearest hundred.

4. At Rosewood Elementary, there are 369 students who have blue eyes.

5. The city of Daviston has 720 teachers.

6. In Marc's school, 412 students have pets.

Round each number to the nearest thousand.

7. Newton County has a population of 4,700.

8. Randy's school has 2,230 people with blonde hair.

16

Pet Pals

Emmett is helping his brother in the pet store after school. Help him find the answer to each problem.

1. Emmett is going to feed the rabbits. There are 11 cages with 4 rabbits in each cage. How many rabbits will Emmett need to feed?

$$\begin{array}{r} 11 \\ \underline{\times\ 4} \\ \textbf{44 rabbits} \end{array}$$

2. The pet store sells 2 times as many red pet collars as blue pet collars. Emmett sells 42 blue pet collars. How many red pet collars does Emmett sell?

3. The pet store has 21 turtles. Emmett feeds 2 lettuce leaves to each turtle. How many lettuce leaves does Emmett feed the turtles?

4. Emmett helps take the dogs for a walk. The pet store has 3 times as many poodles as cocker spaniels. It has 13 cocker spaniels. How many poodles does the pet store have?

5. Emmett is ordering more canary seed for the pet store. If the canaries eat 4 bags of seed in a month, how many bags will Emmett need to order for the next 12 months?

Did you know?

While a cat is sleeping, its body temperature drops slightly. This explains why some cats like to sleep next to their owner or in the sunlight where it is warmer.

1-932210-41-5
Word Problems—Grade 4

Growing and Mowing

Solve each problem.

1. Max needs 48 pounds of grass seed for each lawn he plants. If Max plants 3 lawns, how many pounds of grass seed will he need?

   $$\begin{array}{r} 2 \\ 48 \\ \times\ 3 \\ \hline 144 \end{array}$$ **pounds of grass seed**

2. Spencer is planting tomato plants. He plants 5 rows of 47 tomato plants. How many tomato plants does Spencer plant altogether?

3. Lizzie has 17 watering cans. Each watering can holds 6 gallons of water. How many gallons of water will Lizzie need to fill all 17 watering cans?

4. Jess is putting fertilizer on 23 lawns. He needs 4 bags of fertilizer for each lawn. How many bags of fertilizer will Jess need to buy?

5. Sara is mowing lawns for the summer. She mows 5 lawns a week. If Sara mows lawns for 23 weeks, how many lawns will she mow altogether?

6. Kyle has 3 times as many garden tools as Anne. Anne has 37 garden tools. How many garden tools does Kyle have?

www.skillmill.com   1-932210-41-5

Lemonade Stand

Solve each problem.

1. Jessica uses 16 ounces of sugar in her lemonade recipe. If she makes 9 batches, how much sugar does she need?

$$\begin{array}{r} \overset{5}{16} \\ \times\ 9 \\ \hline 144 \end{array}$$ **ounces**

2. Mario sells 324 glasses of lemonade for 3¢ each. How much money does Mario earn?

3. Jamie sells 21 glasses of lemonade every day. If she sells lemonade for a week, how many glasses will she sell?

4. Tracy has 245 gallons of lemonade. She divides the lemonade into 5-gallon pitchers. How many pitchers can she fill?

5. Samantha buys 27 lemons for 9¢ each. How much money does Samantha spend?

6. Norman has 35 ounces of lemonade. He pours it into 5-ounce cups. How many cups of lemonade does he have?

1-932210-41-5
Word Problems—Grade 4

Solve each problem.

1. The iguanas eat 3 times a week. How many times will Emmett need to feed the iguanas in the next 32 weeks?

2. Emmett sells 3 times as many dog toys as cat toys. Emmett sells 23 cat toys. How many dog toys does Emmett sell?

3. Josh plants 59 squash plants. Each plant has 6 squashes growing on the vine. How many squashes does Josh have?

4. Tyler spends 7¢ each for paper cups. If he buys 1,394 cups, how much money does he spend?

5. Kim sells lemonade for a week. Each day she earns $23.49. How much does she earn for the entire week?

6. Jasmine has 128 ounces of lemonade. She divides it equally into 8-ounce glasses. How many glasses of lemonade does Jasmine have?

www.skillmill.com   1-932210-41-5

Basketball Scores

10

Solve each problem.

Remember...
- The <u>range</u> is the difference between the highest number and the lowest number in the data.
- To calculate the <u>mean</u> (or average), add the list of numbers and then divide by the number of items.
- The <u>median</u> is the middle number that appears in the data.
- The <u>mode</u> is the number that appears most often in the data.

The Panthers kept track of their scores from their last seven basketball games.
<u>Here are their scores:</u>
93,   90,   85,   85,   81,   71,   69

1. What is the range of the basketball scores?

2. What is the mode of the basketball scores?

3. What is the median of the basketball scores?

4. What is the mean of the basketball scores?

Did you know?

Michael Jordan was the NBA scoring leader for ten seasons. In 1987, Michael Jordan earned an average of 37.1 points per game.

Answer the following questions using the graphs below.

Points Scored at the Playoff Game

This is a bar graph. There is one bar for each person. Teresa and her friends played in the playoff basketball game for their school. The graph shows how many points they earned for their team.

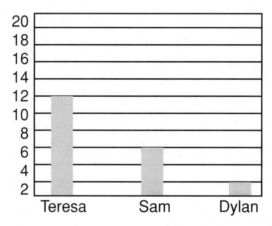

1. How many points did Sam score? _____

2. How many more points did Teresa score than Dylan? _____

3. How many points did Sam, Teresa, and Dylan score altogether? _____

4. How many points are represented by each line on the bar graph? _____

Two Scoops, Please

Use the circle graph to answer the questions.

Lisa's class members voted on their favorite flavors of ice cream. Use the circle graph to answer the questions below.

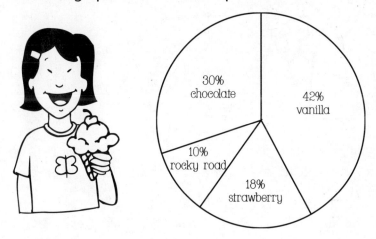

1. Which flavor of ice cream received the highest number of votes?

2. What percentage of students voted for strawberry ice cream as their favorite flavor?

3. Which flavor of ice cream did 10 percent of the students vote for as their favorite?

4. What was the total percentage of students that liked either chocolate or strawberry best?

1-932210-41-5
Word Problems—Grade 4

Two Scoops, Please

Use the line graph to answer the questions.

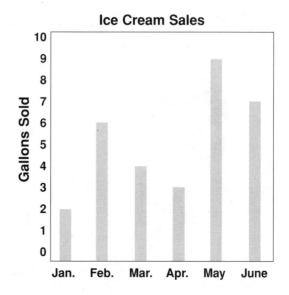

Ice Cream Sales

1. How many gallons of ice cream were sold in January?

   2 gallons

2. Which month had the highest sales?

3. In which month were 4 gallons sold?

4. Which month had the lowest sales?

5. What was the total number of gallons of ice cream sold in February and March?

www.skillmill.com

1-932210-41-5

Graph It!

The chart below shows the number of items sold at Sporty's Sporting Goods store. Put the information in a bar graph.

Item	Number Sold
Basketballs	18
Tennis Rackets	15
Baseballs	12
Bats	12
Gloves	6

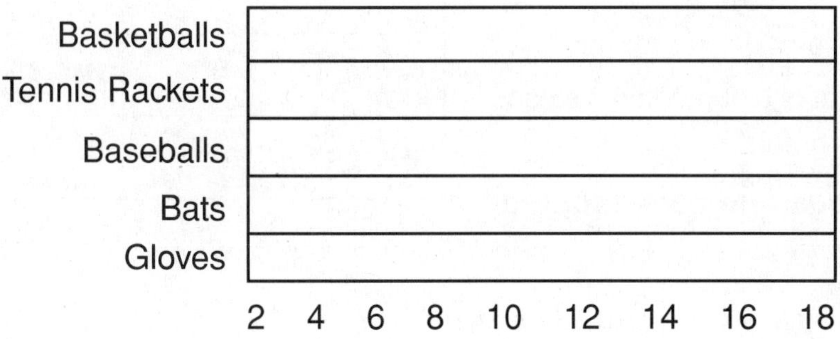

Basketballs	
Tennis Rackets	
Baseballs	
Bats	
Gloves	

2 4 6 8 10 12 14 16 18

Use the bar graph to answer the questions.

1. How many tennis rackets were sold?

2. Which two items had equal numbers sold?

3. How many more basketballs than baseballs were sold?

25

Answer each question using the graph.

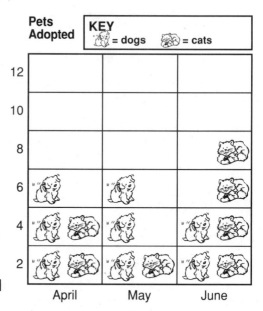

Pets Adopted

KEY: = dogs   = cats

1. What is being compared on this graph?

   dogs and cats adopted

2. How many cats were adopted in April?

3. How many dogs were adopted in June?

4. In which month were the most cats adopted?

5. How many more dogs than cats were adopted in May?

www.skillmill.com

1-932210-41-5

Adopt-a-Pet

Answer each question using the graph.

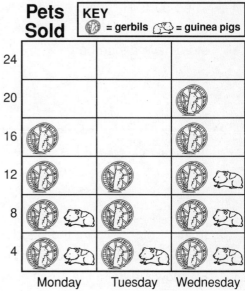

Pets Sold

KEY
🐹 = gerbils 🐹 = guinea pigs

Pets Sold	Monday	Tuesday	Wednesday
24			
20			gerbils
16	gerbils		gerbils
12	gerbils	gerbils	gerbils, guinea pigs
8	gerbils, guinea pigs	gerbils	gerbils, guinea pigs
4	gerbils, guinea pigs	gerbils, guinea pigs	gerbils, guinea pigs

1. What is being compared on this graph?

2. How many gerbils did the pet store sell on Tuesday?

3. On which day of the week were the most gerbils sold?

4. What was the total number of gerbils and guinea pigs sold on Wednesday?

5. On which day of the week did the pet store sell 8 guinea pigs?

1-932210-41-5

Word Problems—Grade 4

Sports-R-Us

Solve each problem.

1. The Sports-R-Us store sells 2 types of tennis rackets. They have 58 of each type of tennis racket. How many tennis rackets does the store have altogether?

$$\overset{1}{5}8$$
$$\underline{\times\ 2}$$
116 tennis rackets

2. Jack saw 4 times as many footballs as soccer balls in the store. Jack saw 34 soccer balls. How many footballs did Jack see?

3. In the winter season, the Sports-R-Us store sells 5 times as many snowboards as it sells during the summer season. The store sells 32 snowboards in the summer season. How many snowboards does the store sell in the winter season?

4. For each display, Tiffany put out 13 dumbbells. If there were 8 different displays, how many dumbbells did Tiffany put out?

5. Steven is checking his inventory. In the spring, he has 3 times as many pairs of skates as in the winter. If Steven has 56 pairs of skates in the winter, how many pairs of skates does he have in the spring?

www.skillmill.com

1-932210-41-5

Solve each problem.

1. Casey sells 1,439 magazines every month. How many magazines does Casey sell in 9 months?

$$\begin{array}{r} {\scriptstyle 3\ 3\ 8} \\ \mathbf{1,439} \\ \underline{\times\ \ 9} \\ \mathbf{12,951}\ \textbf{magazines} \end{array}$$

2. Kyle is a reporter for a magazine. He writes 5 articles that each have 598 words. How many words does Kyle write altogether?

3. Webster is a photographer for a magazine. The magazine uses 2 of his pictures on each page. If there are 139 pages in the magazine, how many pictures will Webster need to give them?

4. The Magazine Shop sold 8 times as many magazines as Montgomery's Bookstore. If Montgomery's Bookstore sold 2,587 magazines, how many magazines did the Magazine Shop sell?

5. Monica stocks shelves in the magazine store and puts 7 magazines in each box. Monica has 342 full boxes. How many magazines does Monica have?

Did you know?

Reader's Digest was the top-selling magazine in the U.S. in the year 2000. The magazine's circulation was 12,566,047. The second most popular magazine was *TV Guide*.

29

Solve each problem.

1. The Sports-R-Us store sold 8 times as many skateboards in June as it sold in September. The store sold 57 skateboards in September. How many skateboards did the store sell in June?

2. Julia sold 6 times as many bicycle helmets as bicycles. Julie sold 18 bicycles. How many bicycle helmets did Julia sell?

3. Coach LaVerde bought 3 times as many baseballs as footballs. If Coach LaVerde bought 28 footballs, how many baseballs did he buy?

4. Ed is a magazine editor. He edits 4 pages each day. How many pages will he edit in 259 days?

5. Diane sells magazine subscriptions. She sells 3,842 subscriptions in one month. How many magazine subscriptions does she sell in 9 months?

www.skillmill.com

1-932210-41-5

And the Winner Is...

Solve each problem.

1. The California candidate got 34 times more votes than the Florida candidate. The Florida candidate got 85 votes. How many votes did the California candidate get?

> If I am elected president, I promise to outlaw peas!

$$\begin{array}{r} {}^{1}{}^{2}85 \\ \times\ 34 \\ \hline 340 \\ \underline{255\ \ } \\ \textbf{2,890}\ \textbf{votes} \end{array}$$

2. Twenty-seven students voted for Arthur. Thirty-one times more students voted for Webster. How many students voted for Webster?

3. Amy polled her class to see what the class's favorite kind of pizza was. Thirteen times more students voted for pepperoni pizza than cheese pizza. Sixteen students voted for cheese pizza. How many students voted for pepperoni pizza?

4. Chad was elected president of the Wildlife Preservation Club. He got 56 times more votes than his opponent. If his opponent got 368 votes, how many votes did Chad get?

Did you know?

Three U.S. presidents died on July 4: John Adams, Thomas Jefferson, and James Monroe.

1-932210-41-5

Word Problems—Grade 4

Bookworm Bonanza

Solve each problem.

1. Hillary reads 842 pages a week. How many pages will Hillary read in 9 weeks?

$$\begin{array}{r} {\scriptstyle 3\ 1} \\ \mathbf{842} \\ \mathbf{x\ \ \ 9} \\ \hline \mathbf{7{,}578}\ \textbf{pages} \end{array}$$

2. Each day, 328 people come to the library. How many people will come to the library in a week?

3. Each magazine box holds 9 magazines. The library has 528 full magazine boxes. How many magazines does the library have?

4. Gary checked out 467 books in a year. Kristen checked out 3 times as many books as Gary. How many books did Kristen check out?

5. The Southtown Library has 8 times as many books as the Littleton Library. The Littleton Library has 356 books. How many books does the Southtown Library have?

Did you know?

In the year 2000, a total of 23.3 million Harry Potter books were sold in the United States.

1-932210-41-5

Solve each problem.

1. Jonathan delivers 9 newspapers. He gets paid $1.14 for each newspaper he delivers. How much money does Jonathan earn?

$$\begin{array}{r} \overset{1\ 3}{\$1.14} \\ \times\ 9 \\ \hline \$10.26 \end{array}$$

2. Annie places an ad in the newspaper. The newspaper charges 5¢ a word. Annie's ad has 694 words. How much does the ad cost Annie?

3. Desi spends $34.56 at the newsstand. Meg spends $58.31 at the newsstand. How much more money did Meg spend than Desi?

4. The *Daily Times* sells 3,491 newspapers for 4¢ each. How much money does the *Daily Times* make?

5. Tara buys 2 newspapers that cost $3.95 each. She gives the clerk $10.00. How much change does Tara get back?

6. Belle gets paid 9¢ for each word she writes. Belle writes 4,593 words. How much money does Belle earn?

1-932210-41-5
Word Problems—Grade 4

Solve each problem.

1. Isabella buys 9 balloons for 35¢ each. How much does she spend in all?

$$\begin{array}{r} 4 \\ .35 \\ \underline{\times\ 9} \\ \mathbf{\$3.15} \end{array}$$

2. Tyler, Ann, and Jason want to get their faces painted. Face painting costs 69¢. How much money will the 3 of them need to have their faces painted?

3. Carl buys 256 tickets for 3¢ each. How much does he spend on tickets?

4. Charlotte rides the Spin-a-Whirl 19 times. If 1 ride costs 5¢, how much does Charlotte spend on Spin-a-Whirl rides altogether?

5. Jess buys 146 pieces of candy for 6¢ each. How much does he spend in all?

6. T-shirts cost $18 each. Amy buys 7 T-shirts. How much does Amy spend on T-shirts?

Solve each problem.

1. Alex buys 7 chocolate chip cookies for $1.24. How much does Alex spend on cookies?

$$\begin{array}{r} {\scriptstyle 1\ 2} \\ \$1.24 \\ \times\ \ \ 7 \\ \hline \$8.68 \end{array}$$

2. Jennifer works in a bakery. She earns $5.85 an hour. If Jennifer works 8 hours a day, how much does she earn in one day?

3. Luiz buys 9 cakes for $16.48 each. How much money does Luiz spend?

4. Shelly spends 6 times as much on pies for her party as Tom does. Tom spends $24.83. How much does Shelly spend on pies?

5. Madison, Gary, and Annie each buy one dozen doughnuts. One dozen doughnuts costs $7.59. How much do they spend on doughnuts altogether?

Did you know?

During the Civil War, the Bureau of Engraving and Printing printed paper money in denominations of 3 cents, 5 cents, 10 cents, 25 cents, and 50 cents. Paper money was printed when people hoarded coins, creating a drastic coin shortage.

Solve each problem.

Remember…
The perimeter is the distance around a figure. To find the perimeter of a figure, add up the lengths of each side of the figure.

1. Jeremy is building a dog pen. Two of the sides are 17 feet long, and the other two sides are 21 feet long.
How much fencing will Jeremy need?

$$\begin{array}{r} {}^{1}17 \\ 21 \\ 17 \\ +\ 21 \\ \hline 76 \end{array}$$ **feet of fencing**

2. Heather is putting tile around the edge of her swimming pool. Her swimming pool measures 20 feet by 16 feet. How many feet of tile will Heather have to put down?

3. Beth needs enough ribbon to go around the perimeter of her blanket. If the blanket measures 45 inches by 60 inches, how many inches of ribbon will Beth need to buy?

4. Kim is fencing an area in her yard. If two of the edges are 45 feet, and the other two edges are 57 feet, how many feet of fencing will Kim need?

Did you know?

U.S. currency measures 2.61 inches wide by 6.14 inches long and is .0043 inches thick. If the bills printed each year were laid end to end, they would stretch around the earth's equator approximately 24 times. Larger-sized notes in circulation before 1929 measured 3.125 inches by 7.4218 inches.

www.skillmill.com   1-932210-41-5

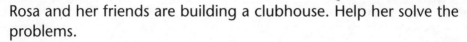
Rosa and her friends are building a clubhouse. Help her solve the problems.

Remember…
To find the area of a rectangular figure, multiply the length by the width.

1. Rosa and Mike need to figure the area of the floor so they know how many boards to buy. If the floor is 8 feet by 12 feet, what is the area of the floor?

$$\begin{array}{r} {}^{1}12 \\ \times\ 8 \\ \hline 96 \end{array}$$ **square feet**

2. Amy measures the area for the window. The window measures 16 inches wide and 21 inches tall. What is the area of the window?

3. Dylan wants to paint the back door to the clubhouse. The door is 56 inches tall and 32 inches wide. What is the area of the door?

4. Mike and Haley are working on the roof. They need to figure out the area so they will know how many supplies to buy. The roof is 108 inches by 156 inches. What is the area of the clubhouse roof?

5. Ashley wants to carpet a space in the clubhouse that is 32 inches by 59 inches. What is the area of the space she wants to carpet?

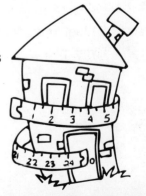

37

Solve each problem.

1. Max is making a frame for a picture he painted. The picture is 36 inches by 18 inches. How many inches will his finished frame be?

2. Lizzy is making a garden in her yard. What is the perimeter of her garden if each edge measures 36 feet?

3. Nancy is sewing trim around a tablecloth. If the tablecloth is 108 inches long and 72 inches wide, how many inches of trim does Nancy need?

4. Rosa makes a small flower garden outside the clubhouse. The garden is 23 meters wide and 37 meters long. What is the area of Rosa's garden?

5. Dylan plants grass in an area behind the clubhouse that is 14 feet wide and 54 feet long. What is the area that Dylan plants?

Solve each problem.

1. The fourth grade is going on a field trip to the zoo. There are 108 students and 3 buses. How many students are on each bus?

   108 ÷ 3 = 36 students

2. The class visits the reptile house at the zoo. There are 245 reptiles. Each cage holds 5 reptiles. How many cages are there?

3. Robin's class takes a field trip to the museum. Robin sees 116 exhibits total. Each room has 4 exhibits in it. How many rooms does Robin go through?

4. Adrian's class is going to the theater. Half of the group goes into theater A. The other half of the group goes into theater B. If there are 114 students, how many students are in each theater?

5. Dan's class visits the natural history museum. The class sees 222 relics. If there are 6 relics in each room, how many rooms does the museum have?

Did you know?

Star Wars: Episode I—The Phantom Menace earned 431 million dollars in ticket sales. *Toy Story 2* earned 245.9 million dollars, and *The Lion King* earned 312.9 million dollars in ticket sales.

1-932210-41-5
Word Problems—Grade 4

Fantastic Flowers

Solve each problem.

1. Pam's favorite flowers are daisies. Pam spends $7.88 on 4 bunches of daisies. How much does each bunch cost?

$$7.88 \div 4 = \$1.97$$

2. Todd buys 7 long-stem roses. Todd spends $6.51 on the roses. How much does each rose cost?

3. Jada wants some purple flowers. She buys a 6-pack of petunias for $4.32. How much does each petunia plant cost?

4. The plant nursery has a sale on geraniums. Lance buys a case with 9 geraniums for $12.51. How much does each geranium cost?

5. Marie buys an 8-pound bag of plant fertilizer for $19.92. What is the cost per pound for the plant fertilizer?

6. Penny wants some marigold plants. She spends $18.41 on 7 potted marigolds. How much does each potted marigold cost?

1-932210-41-5

Solve each problem.

1. Heather's class goes to a farm. At the farm, the class goes for a wagon ride. There are 105 students. If the wagon holds 7 students, how many trips will the wagon need to make so everyone gets a ride?

2. At the history museum, Danny's class breaks up into groups of 8 to look at the exhibits. If there are 168 students, how many groups are there?

3. There are 416 students who go to the movie theater. Each row seats 8 people. How many rows does the theater need to seat everyone?

4. Eric needs a big bag of dirt. He finds a 5-pound bag of dirt on sale for $7.80. What is the cost per pound for the bag of dirt?

5. Brittany likes tall plants. She buys a 4-pack of sunflower plants for $3.04. How much does Brittany spend for each sunflower plant?

I'm growing a row of numbers.

1-932210-41-5

Word Problems—Grade 4

Solve each problem.

1. Marcy buys rulers for her class. Each box has 8 rulers. How many boxes does Marcy need if there are 85 students in her class?

$$85 \div 8 = 10 + \text{remainder of } 5$$
$$\textbf{11 boxes}$$

2. Craig has $37. He buys bottles of glue for $2 each. How many bottles of glue can Craig buy?

3. Justin buys notebooks for all 159 students in his class. If each carton contains 7 notebooks, how many cartons does Justin need to buy to give one notebook to each student?

4. Penny brings candy for the class. Each package of candy has 9 pieces. There are 67 students in her class. How many packages of candy does Penny need to bring?

5. Sam shares stickers with his class. Each sticker sheet has 5 stickers. If Sam's class has 32 people, how many sheets of stickers does Sam need?

Did you know?

The Bureau of Engraving and Printing produces 37 million bills a day with a face value of approximately $696 million. Forty-five percent of the notes printed are $1 bills.

Solve each problem.

1. The hotel has 243 rooms. If each floor has 27 rooms, how many floors are in the hotel?

   243 ÷ 27 = 9 floors

2. James and his friends are at the Rent-a-Car lot. Rent-a-Car has 392 cars. Each row has 56 cars. How many rows of cars are on the lot?

3. Kim flies to California. On her flight, there are 144 passengers and 48 rows of seats. How many seats are in each row?

4. Lucy and her friends eat lunch at an Italian restaurant. The restaurant can seat 190 people. If there are 38 tables, how many people does each table seat?

5. Abby and her friends are visiting an amusement park. Their favorite ride, the Tidal Wave, holds 74 people. If 2 people fit in a car, how many cars are there on the ride?

Say, "Math vacation!"

43

Solve each problem.

1. Chloe has $15 to spend on pencils. Each box of pencils costs $2. How many boxes of pencils can Chloe buy? How much money does Chloe have left after she buys the pencils?

2. There are 149 people in Ross's class. Ross buys erasers for each of the students. Erasers are sold 4 to a package. How many packages of erasers does Ross need to buy?

3. Janice has $269 to spend on books. Each book costs $8. How many books can Janice buy?

4. Jan buys 66 postcards to send to her friends. If she sends postcards to 33 friends, how many postcards will each friend get?

5. Thomas and his friends go to a football game. There are 774 fans at the game. If there are 86 rows of seats, how many seats are in each row?

6. Max is waiting for his tour bus. Each bus can carry 47 tourists. If there are 282 tourists, how many tour buses are there?

www.skillmill.com

1-932210-41-5

Party Planning

Solve each problem.

1. Samantha bakes 252 cupcakes for her birthday party. She gives each guest a box with 4 cupcakes. How many boxes does she have?

   252 ÷ 4 = 63 boxes

2. Jill buys 349 party favors for 7¢ each. How much does Jill spend?

3. Bill has 72 cans of soda in 6-packs. How many 6-packs does he have?

4. A bunch of 12 balloons costs $13.99. If Marissa buys 3 bunches, how much does she spend on balloons?

5. Vivian has 396 party hats. Each package contains 6 party hats. How many packages of party hats does Vivian have?

6. Amanda puts up decorations. She has 224 inches of ribbon and needs to cut 7-inch pieces. How many 7-inch pieces can she cut?

Are We There Yet?

Chloe and her family are taking a vacation. Help her solve the following problems.

1. Chloe's family waits for her brother to get home. It's 6:00, and they wait for 30 minutes. What time is it now?

6:30

2. Chloe's family leaves at 7:15. They drive for 30 minutes and then stop for dinner. What time is it when they stop for dinner?

3. At 8:45, Chloe asks how much longer it will take to get to their hotel. Her mom says it will take 1 hour and 30 minutes more. What time will they reach their hotel?

4. At 9:00, Chloe's little brother needs to stop for a break. The family stops for 15 minutes. What time do they get back on the road again?

5. Chloe sets her alarm clock for 7:15 in the morning. She oversleeps 30 minutes. What time does Chloe get up?

www.skillmill.com

1-932210-41-5

Measuring Up

Solve each problem.

Remember...
- *If you change a larger unit to a smaller unit (yards to feet), you multiply.*
- *If you change a smaller unit to a larger unit (inches to feet), you divide.*
  - *12 inches = 1 foot*
  - *3 feet = 1 yard*
  - *36 inches = 1 yard*

1. Pam needs 36 inches of rope. How many yards does she need to buy?

$$36 \div 12 = 3 \text{ feet} = 1 \text{ yard}$$

2. Jason needs 180 inches of string for his project. How many yards should he buy?

3. Maggie is carpeting her hall. The length of the hall is 14 feet. Carpet is sold by the yard. How many yards does Maggie need to buy so she will have enough?

4. Kristen is going to put together a puzzle that is 72 inches wide. Her table is 5 feet wide. How many inches wide is Kristen's table? Will her puzzle fit on the table?

5. The toy racetrack is 60 inches long. How many feet is the toy racetrack?

1-932210-41-5

Kitchen Conversions

Solve each problem.

Remember…
- *If you change a larger unit to a smaller unit (tablespoon to teaspoon), you multiply.*
- *If you change a smaller unit to a larger unit (quart to gallon), you divide.*

      1 tablespoon = 3 teaspoons
      1 pint = 2 cups
      1 quart = 2 pints
      1 gallon = 4 quarts
      1 pound = 16 ounces

1. Maria's jam recipe calls for 8 pints of chopped fruit. How many quarts of chopped fruit does she need?

$$8 \div 2 = \textbf{4 quarts}$$

2. Ben needs 16 quarts of punch for the party. How many gallons of punch does Ben need to buy?

3. James is making cookies for a bake sale at his school. He uses 64 ounces of chocolate chips in his recipe. How many pounds of chocolate chips does he use?

4. Mario needs 3 gallons of soup for his party. The restaurant packages his soup in quart bottles. How many bottles does he have to pick up?

www.skillmill.com   1-932210-41-5

Measuring & Conversion Review

Solve each problem.

1. Andrea buys 7 yards of fabric. How many feet of fabric does she have?

2. Stuart is 5 feet 9 inches tall. How many inches tall is Stuart?

3. Mike's garage is 22 feet long. His car is 108 inches long and his trailer is 140 inches long. How long is Mike's car and trailer altogether? Will both the car and trailer fit in the garage?

4. Angela is making a triple-layer chocolate cake, and her recipe calls for 2 tablespoons of vanilla. Angela only has a teaspoon to measure with. How many teaspoons should she use?

5. Dennis is making salsa for his friends. He has 32 cups of salsa and puts it in 1-pint jars. How many 1-pint jars does Dennis need?

6. Chloe is excited to get to the amusement park. The family reaches the amusement park at 8:00 A.M. They wait in line to get in for 45 minutes. What time is it when they go inside the park?

Solve each problem.

Remember...
When the denominators are the same, subtract the numerators and then the whole numbers.

1. Duane watches a car race. The red race car drives $7\frac{1}{10}$ miles. The silver race car drives $9\frac{6}{10}$ miles. How many more miles does the silver race car drive than the red race car?

$$9\frac{6}{10}$$
$$-\ 7\frac{1}{10}$$
$$\overline{\mathbf{2\frac{5}{10}\ miles}}$$

2. The brown horse runs $\frac{3}{12}$ of a mile farther than the black horse. The black horse runs $15\frac{4}{12}$ of a mile. How far does the brown horse run?

3. Karla runs $6\frac{5}{16}$ miles, and Jason runs $11\frac{4}{16}$ miles. How many miles do Karla and Jason run altogether?

4. Toby competes in a bicycle race. On the first day of the race, he rides $17\frac{4}{23}$ miles. On the second day of the race, he rides $22\frac{12}{23}$ miles. How far does Toby ride altogether?

5. John runs $10\frac{3}{6}$ meters. Erica runs $11\frac{5}{6}$ meters. How much farther does Erica run?

Did you know?

The average speed of a car driving in the Indianapolis 500 race in 2001 was 131.294 miles per hour.

Birthday Blast

Ryan is making a birthday cake for his friend's birthday. Help him solve each problem.

Remember...
When adding or subtracting fractions with different denominators, first find the lowest common denominator for the fractions. Convert the fractions, and then add or subtract the numerators.

1. Ryan needs $6\frac{3}{4}$ cups of flour for his recipe. When he measures the flour in his bag, he only has $3\frac{2}{3}$ cups of flour. How much more flour does Ryan need for his recipe?

$$6\frac{3}{4} = \qquad 6\frac{9}{12}$$
$$-3\frac{2}{3} = \qquad -3\frac{8}{12}$$
$$\overline{\qquad\qquad\qquad \mathbf{3\frac{1}{12}\ \text{cups of flour}}}$$

2. Next, the recipe says to sift together $\frac{5}{8}$ teaspoon of baking powder with $\frac{1}{3}$ teaspoon of salt. How many teaspoons does Ryan sift altogether?

3. Ryan adds $1\frac{2}{3}$ cups of sugar and realizes he put in too much sugar. He takes out $\frac{1}{4}$ cup of sugar from the mixing bowl. How much sugar did Ryan use in the recipe?

4. Applesauce is the next ingredient Ryan needs to add. He measures $\frac{5}{8}$ cup and then adds $\frac{1}{9}$ cup. How much applesauce did Ryan add altogether?

5. Ryan has a full carton of 12 eggs. He uses $\frac{1}{3}$ of the carton. How many eggs does Ryan have left?

1-932210-41-5
Word Problems—Grade 4

Solve each problem.

1. Mindy drives her car $35\frac{6}{12}$ times around the racetrack. Shannon drives her car $21\frac{4}{12}$ times around the racetrack. How many more times does Mindy drive her car around the racetrack than Shannon does?

2. Jay swims $\frac{3}{10}$ of a mile farther than Randy. If Randy swims $2\frac{4}{10}$ miles, how far does Jay swim?

3. Mario wins the race by $\frac{2}{12}$ of a second. If his closest competitor's time was $\frac{11}{12}$ of a second, what was Mario's time?

4. Ryan bakes the cake for $25\frac{5}{12}$ minutes. He decides it needs to bake longer. He bakes it for another $2\frac{3}{6}$ minutes. How long does the cake bake altogether?

5. Next, Ryan frosts the birthday cake. He uses $1\frac{5}{6}$ cups of frosting and then adds another $\frac{3}{8}$ cup of frosting. How much frosting does Ryan use altogether?

6. Last, Ryan puts the candles on the cake. Ryan has a full box of 12 candles. He uses $\frac{5}{6}$ of the box. How many candles does Ryan have left?

www.skillmill.com

1-932210-41-5

Painting Perfect

Solve each problem.

1. Rich bought $\frac{5}{16}$ quart of white paint and $\frac{11}{16}$ quart of blue paint. How much more blue paint did Rich buy?

$$\frac{11}{16} - \frac{5}{16} = \frac{6}{16} \text{ quart blue paint}$$

2. Heidi bought a gallon of paint. She needs $\frac{3}{4}$ of a gallon to paint her garage door. She spills $\frac{2}{4}$ of a gallon of paint. How much more paint does Heidi need to buy so she will have enough?

3. Mitch mixes $\frac{6}{8}$ of a quart of pink paint with $\frac{1}{8}$ of a quart of white paint. How much paint does he end up with?

4. Maria is at the paint store buying paintbrushes. She notices that $\frac{7}{10}$ of the paintbrushes are large, and $\frac{3}{10}$ of the paintbrushes are small. How many more large paintbrushes are there than small paintbrushes?

5. Daisy needs $\frac{8}{12}$ of a quart of paint to paint her backyard fence. She buys 1 quart of paint at the paint store. How much paint will Daisy have left?

My favorite color is purple!

1-932210-41-5
Word Problems—Grade 4

Solve each problem.

1. Meg sold 8,397 tickets at the fair. Sam sold 5 times as many tickets as Meg. How many tickets did Sam sell?

$$\begin{array}{r} {\scriptstyle 1\ 4\ 3} \\ \mathbf{8,397} \\ \underline{\times\qquad \mathbf{5}} \\ \mathbf{41,985}\ \textbf{tickets} \end{array}$$

2. There were 69 jars of pickles at the pickle-judging contest. Each jar had 9 pickles in it. How many pickles were there altogether?

3. The state fair is open for 9 weeks. How many days is that?

4. Mitch buys a soda for $1.45 and a hamburger for $3.54. He pays with a 10-dollar bill. How much change does Mitch get back?

5. The Twist-a-Whirl has 15 cars. Each car holds 4 people. How many people can ride the Twist-a-Whirl at a time?

6. Janice sold 7 times as many packages of cotton candy as Tim. Tim sold 3,2&& packages of cotton candy. How many packages of cotton candy did Janice sell?

Going the Distance

Solve each problem.

1. Henry runs three and six-tenths miles. Write the decimal number that shows how many miles Henry runs.

3.6

2. Dotty scores twenty-three and two-tenths points. Write the decimal number that shows how many points Dotty scores.

3. Jacob's kite flies sixty-nine and five-hundredths yards. Write the decimal number that shows how many yards Jacob's kite flies.

4. Becky swims two and thirty-five-hundredths miles. Write the decimal number that shows how many miles Becky swims.

5. Max scored twenty-eight and two-tenths points. Write the decimal number that shows how many points Max scored.

6. Jackson drives fifty-eight and forty-five-hun-dredths miles. Write the decimal number that shows how many miles Jackson drives.

7. Brad throws the ball twenty-one and three-tenths feet. Write the decimal number that shows how many feet Brad throws the ball.

1-932210-41-5   Word Problems—Grade 4

Car Craze

Solve each problem.

Remember...
To add and subtract decimals, you must first line up the decimal points. Put in zeros for
any missing numbers. Add or subtract. Remember to put the decimal point in the answer.

1. Eve drives 67.4 miles farther than Tyler. If Tyler drives 45.39 miles, how many miles does Eve drive?

$$\begin{array}{r} 1 \\ 67.40 \\ + \ 45.39 \\ \hline 112.79 \ \textbf{miles} \end{array}$$

2. In 2000, 47.8 percent of the cars sold in the U.S. were midsize cars. The percentage of small cars sold was 28.1 percent. How many more midsize cars than small cars were sold ?

3. Brett drives 95.3 miles on Friday and 76.9 miles on Saturday. How many miles did Brett drive altogether?

4. In 1999, 16.5 percent of people in the U.S. bought luxury cars. That same year, 52.7 percent of the people in the U.S. bought midsize cars. What was the total percentage of people that bought either luxury cars or midsize cars?

5. Dean's truck gets 15.3 miles per gallon of gas. Christy's car gets 25.2 miles per gallon of gas. How many more miles per gallon does Christy's car get?

www.skillmill.com   1-932210-41-5

Olympic Champions

Solve each problem.

1. In 1996, the best time for the 400-meter hurdles was 47.54 seconds. The best time in 1980 was 48.70 seconds. How much faster
was the time in 1996 than the time in 1980?

$$\begin{array}{r} 48.\overset{6}{\cancel{7}}0 \\ -\ 47.54 \\ \hline \textbf{1.16 seconds} \end{array}$$

2. In the long jump, Carl Lewis had a distance of 8.50 meters in 1996.
In 1936, Jesse Owens had a distance of 8.06 meters. How much
farther than Jesse Owens did Carl Lewis jump?

3. U.S. speed skater Bonnie Blair won the Olympic gold medal for
women's 500-meter speed skating in 1992 and 1994. In 1992, her
time was 40.33 seconds. In 1994, her time was 39.25 seconds.
How much faster was Bonnie's time in 1994 than her time in 1992?

4. In 2000, the 100-meter freestyle was
completed in 48.30 seconds. In 1972, the
100-meter freestyle was completed in
51.22 seconds. How many seconds more
did it take to complete the 100-meter freestyle in
1972?

Use
math
to get
the gold!

Did you know?

The symbol for the Olympic Games is five rings. Each ring symbolizes a conti-
nent: Europe, Asia, Africa, Australia, and America. The blue, yellow, black,
green, and red rings are linked together to represent the friendship of all people.

Solve each problem.

1. Claire jogs six and nine-tenths miles. Write the decimal number that shows how many miles Claire jogs.

2. Mitch earns ten and forty-five-thousandths points. Write the decimal number that shows how many points Mitch earns.

3. Silver was the most popular color of sports car sold in the U.S. in 2000. In that year, 22.3 percent of the sports cars sold were silver, and 14.4 percent of the sports cars sold were black. How many more silver sports cars were sold?

4. The U.S. won gold medals in the women's 100-meter run in both 1996 and 2000. The winning time in 1996 was 10.94 seconds. The winning time in 2000 was 10.75 seconds. How much faster was the winning time in 2000?

5. In 1994, Jean-Luc Brassard won the gold medal in men's moguls freestyle skiing with 27.24 points. In 1998, Jonny Moseley won the gold medal with 26.93 points. How many more points did Brassard have than Moseley?

www.skillmill.com

1-932210-41-5

Answer Pages

Page 3
1. 41 grasshoppers and beetles
2. 53 black ants
3. 59 caterpillars
4. 61 spiders
5. 43 ladybugs

Page 4
1. 831 pounds of food
2. 97 reptiles
3. 6,891 people
4. 111 pictures
5. 6,240 ounces of birdseed

Page 5
1. 37 bees
2. 40 butterflies
3. 150 cages
4. 419 feet
5. 245 animals

Page 6
1. 46 feet
2. 323 feet
3. 73 feet
4. 204 feet

Page 7
1. 18° F
2. 18 inches
3. 27° F
4. 15 miles

Page 8
1. 2,096 cups
2. 5,868 tickets
3. 712 packages
4. 502 tickets
5. 469 seats

Page 9
1. 1,358 tropical fish
2. 7,628 feet
3. 5,425 seashells
4. 2,326 feet
5. 127 sea urchins

Page 10
1. 9,490 feet
2. 8,715 feet
3. 83 feet
4. 523 sea creatures
5. 1,984 fish
6. 1,877 feet

Page 11
1. 5,491 students
2. 198 students
3. 564 students
4. 1,262 students
5. 1,236 students
6. 1,495 students

Page 12
1. $13.68
2. $4.41
3. $7.85
4. $8.63
5. Yes, he has $.95 left.

Page 13
1. $86.30
2. $52.69
3. $43.37
4. $133.20
5. $15.29

Page 14
1. 494 calories
2. 44 calories
3. 378 calories
4. 321 calories
5. 495 calories
6. pizza

Answer Pages

Page 15
1. $16.33
2. $97.85
3. $15.36
4. 19° F difference
5. 419 tickets

Page 16
1. 40
2. 40
3. 20
4. 400
5. 700
6. 400
7. 5,000
8. 2,000

Page 17
1. 44 rabbits
2. 84 red pet collars
3. 42 lettuce leaves
4. 39 poodles
5. 48 bags of seed

Page 18
1. 144 pounds of grass seed
2. 235 tomato plants
3. 102 gallons
4. 92 bags of fertilizer
5. 115 lawns
6. 111 garden tools

Page 19
1. 144 ounces
2. 972¢ or $9.72
3. 147 glasses
4. 49 pitchers
5. 243¢ or $2.43
6. 7 cups

Page 20
1. 96 times
2. 69 dog toys
3. 354 squashes
4. 9,758¢ or $97.58
5. $164.43
6. 16 glasses

Page 21
1. 24
2. 85
3. 85
4. 82

Page 22
1. 6 points
2. 10 points
3. 20 points
4. 2 points

Page 23
1. vanilla
2. 18%
3. rocky road
4. 48%

Page 24
1. 2 gallons
2. May
3. March
4. January
5. 10 gallons

Page 25
1. 15 tennis rackets
2. baseballs and bats
3. 6 more basketballs

Page 26
1. dogs and cats adopted
2. 4 cats
3. 4 dogs
4. June
5. 4 more dogs

www.skillmill.com   1-932210-41-5

Page 27
1. gerbils and guinea pigs sold
2. 12 gerbils
3. Wednesday
4. 32 gerbils and guinea pigs
5. Monday

Page 28
1. 116 tennis rackets
2. 136 footballs
3. 160 snowboards
4. 104 dumbbells
5. 168 skates

Page 29
1. 12,951 magazines
2. 2,990 words
3. 278 pictures
4. 20,696 magazines
5. 2,394 magazines

Page 30
1. 456 skateboards
2. 108 helmets
3. 84 baseballs
4. 1,036 pages
5. 34,578 subscriptions

Page 31
1. 2,890 votes
2. 837 students
3. 208 students
4. 20,608 votes

Page 32
1. 7,578 pages
2. 2,296 people
3. 4,752 magazines
4. 1,401 books
5. 2,848 books

Page 33
1. $10.26
2. 3,470¢ or $34.70
3. $23.75
4. 13,964¢ or $139.64
5. $2.10
6. $413.37

Page 34
1. 315¢ or $3.15
2. 207¢ or $2.07
3. 768¢ or $7.68
4. 95¢ or $0.95
5. 876¢ or $8.76
6. $126

Page 35
1. $8.68
2. $46.80
3. $148.32
4. $148.98
5. $22.77

Page 36
1. 76 feet
2. 72 feet
3. 210 inches
4. 204 feet

Page 37
1. 96 square feet
2. 336 square inches
3. 1,792 square inches
4. 16,848 square inches
5. 1,888 square inches

1-932210-41-5

Answer Pages

Page 38
1. 108 inches
2. 144 feet
3. 360 inches
4. 851 square meters
5. 756 square feet

Page 39
1. 36 students
2. 49 cages
3. 29 rooms
4. 57 students
5. 37 rooms

Page 40
1. $1.97
2. $.93
3. $.72
4. $1.39
5. $2.49
6. $2.63

Page 41
1. 15 trips
2. 21 groups
3. 52 rows
4. $1.56
5. $.76

Page 42
1. 11 boxes
2. 18 bottles
3. 23 cartons
4. 8 packages
5. 7 sheets

Page 43
1. 9 floors
2. 7 rows
3. 3 seats
4. 5 people
5. 37 cars

Page 44
1. 7 boxes with $1.00 left over
2. 38 packages
3. 33 books
4. 2 postcards
5. 9 seats
6. 6 buses

Page 45
1. 63 boxes
2. 2,443¢ or $24.43
3. 12 6-packs
4. $41.97
5. 66 packages
6. 32 pieces of ribbon

Page 46
1. 6:30
2. 7:45
3. 10:15
4. 9:15
5. 7:45

Page 47
1. 1 yard
2. 5 yards
3. 5 yards
4. 60 inches, no
5. 5 feet

Page 48
1. 4 quarts
2. 4 gallons
3. 4 pounds
4. 12 bottles

Page 49
1. 21 feet
2. 69 inches
3. 248 inches, yes
4. 6 teaspoons
5. 16 jars
6. 8:45

www.skillmill.com   1-932210-41-5

Answer Pages

Page 50

1. $2\frac{5}{10}$ miles
2. $15\frac{7}{12}$ miles
3. $17\frac{9}{16}$ miles
4. $39\frac{16}{23}$ miles
5. $1\frac{2}{6}$ meters

Page 51

1. $3\frac{1}{12}$ cups flour
2. $\frac{23}{24}$ teaspoon
3. $\frac{17}{12}$ or $1\frac{5}{12}$ cups
4. $\frac{53}{72}$ cup
5. $\frac{8}{12}$, 8 eggs, or $\frac{2}{3}$ of a carton

Page 52

1. $14\frac{2}{12}$ or $14\frac{1}{6}$ times
2. $2\frac{7}{10}$ miles
3. $\frac{9}{12}$ second
4. $27\frac{11}{12}$ minutes
5. $\frac{53}{24}$ or $2\frac{5}{24}$ cups
6. $\frac{2}{12}$, 2 candles, or $\frac{1}{6}$ of the box

Page 53

1. $\frac{6}{16}$ or $\frac{3}{8}$ quart blue paint
2. $\frac{1}{4}$ gallon
3. $\frac{7}{8}$ quart
4. $\frac{4}{10}$ more large paintbrushes
5. $\frac{4}{12}$ quart

Page 54

1. 41,985 tickets
2. 621 pickles
3. 63 days
4. $5.01
5. 60 people
6. 23,065 packages

Page 55

1. 3.6
2. 23.2
3. 69.05
4. 2.35
5. 28.2
6. 58.45
7. 21.3

Page 56

1. 112.79 miles
2. 19.7 percent
3. 172.2 miles
4. 69.2 percent
5. 9.9 miles per gallon

Page 57

1. 1.16 seconds
2. .44 meters
3. 1.08 seconds
4. 2.92 seconds

Page 58

1. 6.9
2. 10.045
3. 7.9 percent
4. .19 seconds
5. .31 points

1-932210-41-5   Word Problems—Grade 4

Notes

Five things I'm thankful for:

1. _____
2. _____
3. _____
4. _____
5. _____